STAR WARS

EPISODES I, II & III

Instrumental Solos

Project Manager: **Carol Cuellar**
Book Art Layout: **Ernesto Ebanks**
Arranged by **Bill Galliford,**
Ethan Neuburg and **Tod Edmondson**

STAR WARS

EPISODES I, II & III

Instrumental Solos

Project Manager: **Carol Cuellar**
Book Art Layout: **Ernesto Ebanks**
Arranged by **Bill Galliford,**
Ethan Neuburg and **Tod Edmondson**

TITLE	BOOK PAGE NO.

STAR WARS
(Main Title)

Music by
JOHN WILLIAMS

Majestically, steady march (♩ = 108)

4

6

DUEL OF THE FATES

Music by
JOHN WILLIAMS

Maestoso, with great force (♩ = 44)

5 **Allegro (♩ = 152)**

Duel of the Fates - 8 - 1
IFM0527CD

11

14

QUI-GON'S FUNERAL

By
JOHN WILLIAMS

Dirge, solemnly (♩ = 60)

Qui-Gon's Funeral - 2 - 1
IFM0527CD

AUGIE'S GREAT MUNICIPAL BAND

By
JOHN WILLIAMS

Augie's Great Municipal Band - 4 - 1
IFM0527CD

20

Augie's Great Municipal Band - 4 - 3
IFM0527CD

41

ACROSS THE STARS
(LOVE THEME FROM *STAR WARS*®: EPISODE II)

Music by
JOHN WILLIAMS

Moderately slow & gently (♩ = 76)

(with pedal)

legato

Across the Stars - 6 - 1
IFM0527CD

Across the Stars - 6 - 2
IFM0527CD

25

Across the Stars - 6 - 4
IFM0527CD

* The cue note represents a more challenging performance alternative.

THE IMPERIAL MARCH
(Darth Vader's Theme)

Music by
JOHN WILLIAMS

The Imperial March - 3 - 1
IFM0527CD

VIOLIN

LEVEL 2–3

STAR WARS
EPISODES I, II & III
Instrumental Solos

THE PHANTOM MENACE™

ATTACK OF THE CLONES®

REVENGE OF THE SITH™

STAR WARS
(Main Title)

Music by
JOHN WILLIAMS

Majestically, steady march (♩ = 108)

IFM0527CD

DUEL OF THE FATES

Music by
JOHN WILLIAMS

Duel of the Fates - 2 - 1
IFM0527CD

QUI-GON'S FUNERAL

By
JOHN WILLIAMS

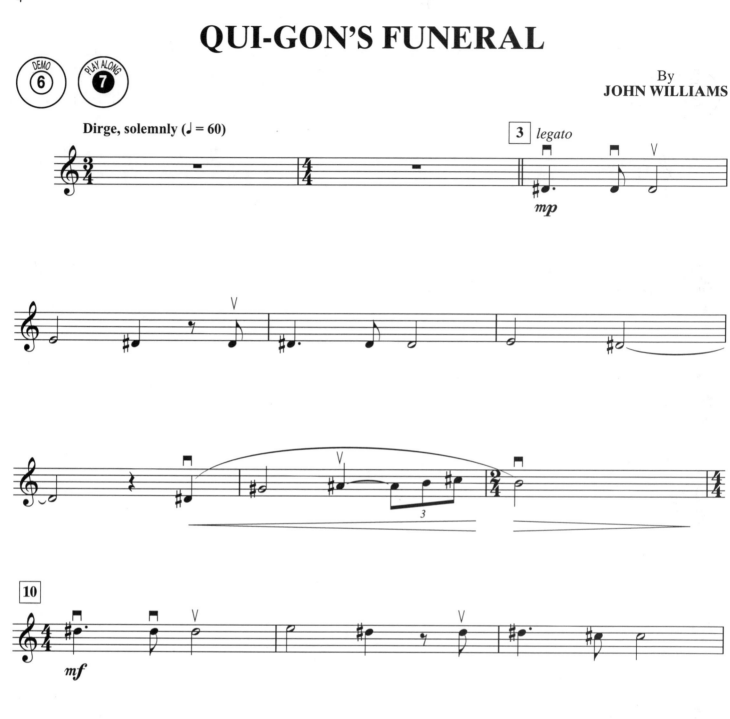

IFM0527CD

AUGIE'S GREAT MUNICIPAL BAND

By
JOHN WILLIAMS

ACROSS THE STARS
(LOVE THEME FROM *STAR WARS*®: EPISODE II)

Music by
JOHN WILLIAMS

Moderately slow & gently (♩ = 76)

Across the Stars - 2 - 1
IFM0527CD

*The cue notes represent a more challenging performance alternative.

THE IMPERIAL MARCH
(Darth Vader's Theme)

Music by
JOHN WILLIAMS

8

THE MEADOW PICNIC

Music by
JOHN WILLIAMS

Moderately slow and flowing (♩. = 50)

*E♯ = F♮

IFM0527CD

MAY THE FORCE BE WITH YOU

Music by
JOHN WILLIAMS

PRINCESS LEIA'S THEME

Music by
JOHN WILLIAMS

*The cue notes below represent an easier alternative.

IFM0527CD

BATTLE OF THE HEROES

Music by
JOHN WILLIAMS

Battle of the Heroes - 2 - 1
IFM0527CD

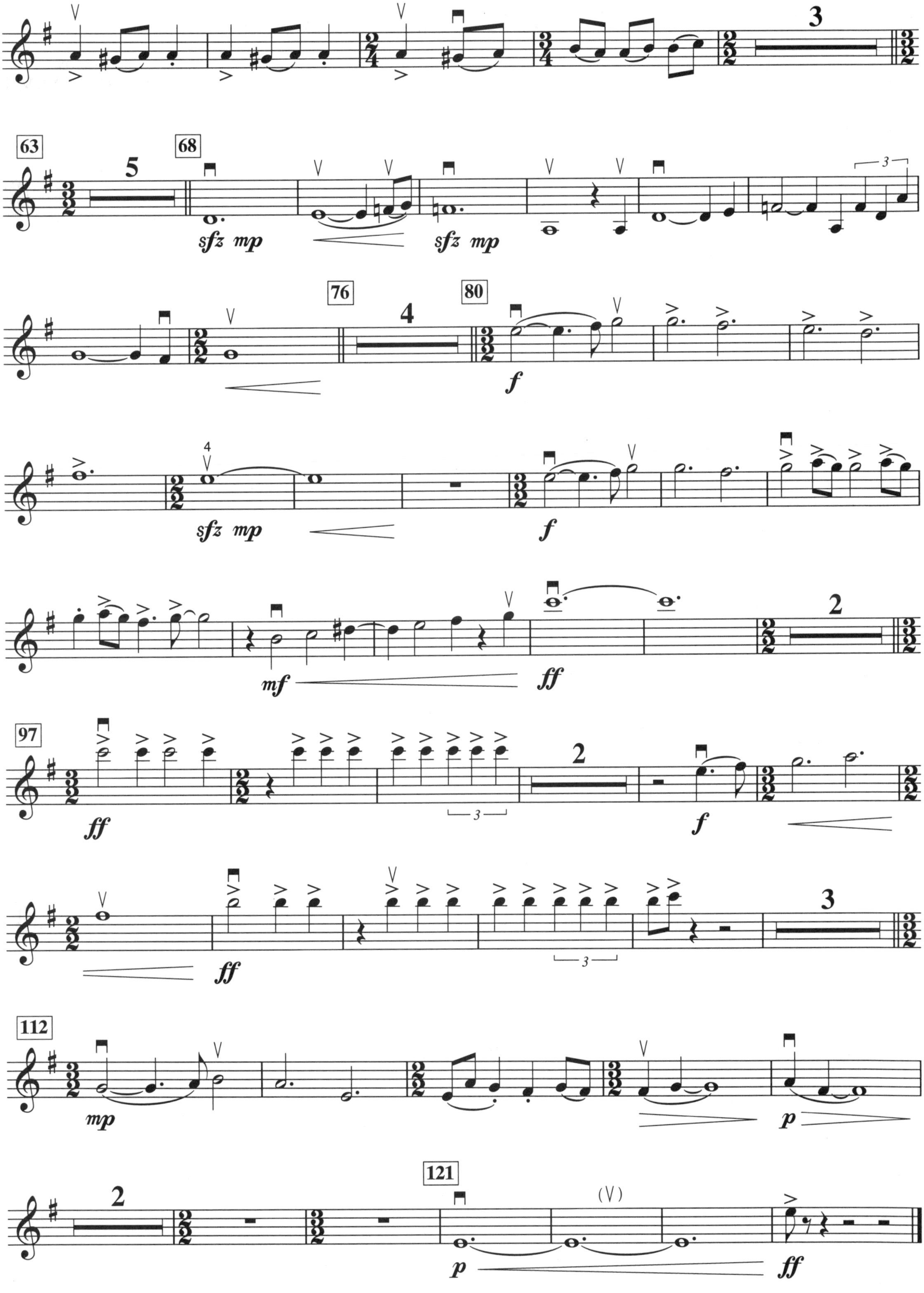
63
68
sfz mp
sfz mp
76
80
f
4
sfz mp
f
mf
ff
97
ff
f
ff
112
mp
p
121
p
ff

THE THRONE ROOM

Music by
JOHN WILLIAMS

* E♯ = F♮
** B♯ = C♮

The Throne Room - 2 - 1
IFM0527CD

The Throne Room - 2 - 2
IFM0527CD

The Imperial March - 3 - 2
IFM0527CD

THE MEADOW PICNIC

Music by
JOHN WILLIAMS

Moderately slow and flowing (♩. = 50)

(with pedal)

The Meadow Picnic - 3 - 1
IFM0527CD

32

* E♯ = F♮

The Meadow Picnic - 3 - 3
IFM0527CD

MAY THE FORCE BE WITH YOU

Music by
JOHN WILLIAMS

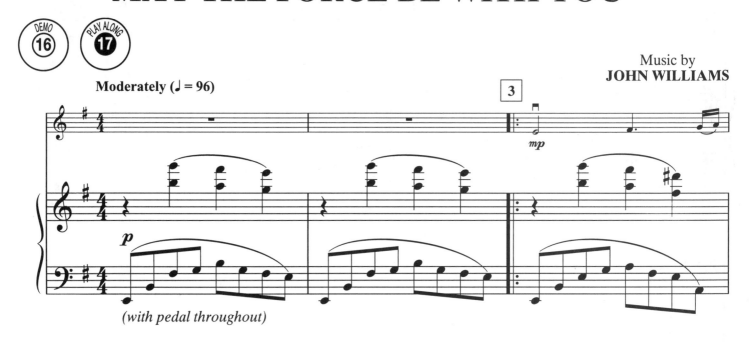

May the Force Be With You - 3 - 1
IFM0527CD

May the Force Be With You - 3 - 3
IFM0527CD

PRINCESS LEIA'S THEME

Music by
JOHN WILLIAMS

Moderately slow, with a gentle flow (♩ = 72)

(with pedal)

Princess Leia's Theme - 3 - 1

IFM0527CD

38

*The cue notes below represent an easier alternative.

Princess Leia's Theme - 3 - 2

IFM0527CD

BATTLE OF THE HEROES

Music by
JOHN WILLIAMS

Maestoso, with great force (♩ = 92)

Battle of the Heroes - 8 - 1
IFM0527CD

42

44

45

Battle of the Heroes - 8 - 6
IFM0527CD

46

Battle of the Heroes - 8 - 7
IFM0527CD

THE THRONE ROOM

Music by
JOHN WILLIAMS

*E♯ = F♮
**B♯ = C♮

The Throne Room - 4 - 1
IFM0527CD

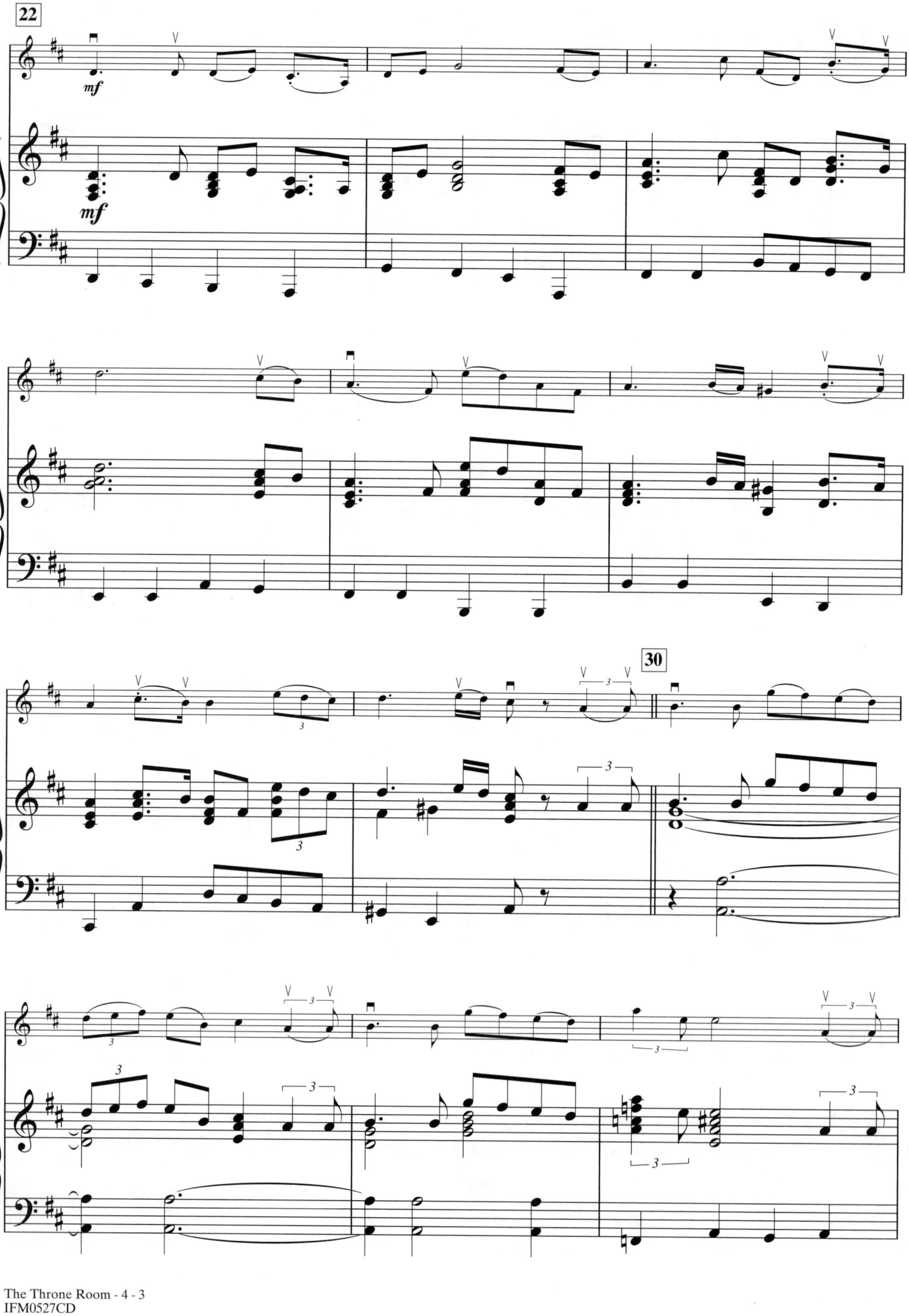
22
mf
mf
30